Original title:
Netted Pearls Beneath the Mermaid Pad

Copyright © 2025 Swan Charm
All rights reserved.

Author: Sara Säde
ISBN HARDBACK: 978-1-80559-478-9
ISBN PAPERBACK: 978-1-80559-977-7

Siren's Serenade of Hidden Depths

In the depths where shadows dance,
Whispers weave a soft romance.
Beneath the waves, secrets call,
A haunting tune, enchanting all.

Rippling echoes through the night,
Voice of sorrow, pure delight.
With every note, the waters sigh,
A tender lure, a lullaby.

Lost souls float in gentle sways,
Caught within the siren's ways.
Heartbeats blend with ocean's flow,
As dreams ignite the depths below.

Her beauty cloaked in twilight's shroud,
Songs of longing, bold and loud.
Yet in her depths, a mystery,
A love ensnared in history.

As tides rise high and whispers dim,
The ocean calls—a silent hymn.
In hidden depths, where shadows play,
The siren sings, then fades away.

Treasures of the Celestial Tide

Under the moonshine bright,
Waves that dance and glide,
Secrets in the starlit night,
Whispers of the celestial tide.

Shells like pearls in hand,
Stories from the sea,
Treasures lost in sands,
Awaiting discovery.

Mysterious creatures roam,
In this tranquil space,
Each wave a tale from home,
A magic we embrace.

Currents sing a song,
Ebbing, flowing low,
In the tides where we belong,
Nature's gentle show.

Dive into the deep,
Feel the ocean's grace,
In dreams, we softly sleep,
On the waves' embrace.

Glittering Echoes of the Deep Sea

Within the ocean's vault,
Where shadows barely creep,
Stars like diamonds salt,
In the water, secrets sleep.

Echoes soft and clear,
Call from depths below,
Whispers that we hear,
On currents they do flow.

Glinting scales like fire,
In the dark they gleam,
Creatures we admire,
Stir from dream to dream.

In this world so vast,
Mysteries abound,
Every wave is cast,
With history profound.

Journey through the night,
Where the silence sings,
In the depths of light,
Hear what the ocean brings.

Underwater Whispers of Wonder

Beneath the azure blue,
Where the water sways,
Life blooms anew,
In a dance that plays.

Coral gardens thrive,
In colors rich and bright,
A world so alive,
In the soft moonlight.

Fish weave through the sea,
In a tapestry rare,
Curious as can be,
In their realm of flair.

Gentle tides embrace,
In a rhythm true,
Nature's quiet grace,
Bids the heart to renew.

Listen to the call,
Of the ocean deep,
In its vastness, we fall,
Underwater, we leap.

The Allure of Forgotten Depths

In the abyssal dark,
Where ancient tales reside,
Lost ships leave their mark,
In the alluring tide.

Forgotten treasures gust,
Amongst the sunken stones,
Whispers turned to rust,
Carry silent tones.

Fragments of a past,
Shimmer in the gloom,
Ghosts of journeys cast,
In the ocean's womb.

Siren songs entice,
In the stillness found,
Lost in their device,
Where secrets cloak the sound.

Dive into the deep,
Where shadows softly play,
In the silence, we keep,
The allure of decay.

Slumbering Beauty in the Tide

In the quiet hush of night,
The waves cradle dreams so light.
Stars above whisper soft and low,
While moonbeams dance on tides below.

Mermaids weave through the crest,
In this haven, they find rest.
A lullaby of ocean's breath,
Embraced by currents, a sweet death.

Coral gardens sway with grace,
Where colors blend, a warm embrace.
Shells collect secrets of the deep,
In slumbering beauty, oceans keep.

With every swell, a tale unfolds,
Of ancient lore and treasures untold.
The seashells whisper of long-lost days,
In the tide's embrace, time gently sways.

Dreamers drift on salty air,
In twilight realms, free from care.
Beneath the stars, the waters glide,
In slumber's peace, the world abides.

A Tidal Symphony of Dreams

Songs of the sea in the night,
Echoing waves, pure delight.
Each crest a note, each trough a pause,
In this symphony, nature's laws.

Gulls cry sweetly in the sky,
As the wind whispers a lullaby.
Melodies rise with the tide's flow,
Painting visions only dreamers know.

Drifting thoughts on the salty breeze,
Carry the whispers of ancient seas.
In every ripple, a harmony found,
A tidal symphony, pure and profound.

Crashing waves join the chorus bright,
As stars twinkle in the dark night.
Carefree hearts in the ocean's sweep,
Lost in dreams, a tranquil deep.

With every ebb, the world unwinds,
A dance of tides, where nature binds.
In the stillness, the soul can glean,
A tidal symphony, serene, unseen.

Sirens Singing Beneath the Surface

In moonlit depths, sirens sway,
With voices soft, they lure and play.
Beneath the waves, their secrets hide,
Enticing sailors, far and wide.

Their songs weave through the ocean's cry,
A haunting melody, a sweet sigh.
Lost in enchantment, hearts betray,
To depths unknown, they drift away.

Glistening scales in the twilight glow,
Reflect the dreams from long ago.
Echoes of longing, soft and sweet,
In the sirens' world, the lost retreat.

With every note, a story spun,
Of love and loss, of battles won.
Drawn to the depths, the brave or bold,
Hear their whispers, legends told.

A shimmering realm beneath the foam,
Where echoes of the heart call home.
In the ocean's grasp, they find their voice,
Sirens singing, the heart's true choice.

The Riddles of the Ocean's Embrace

Whispers of the sea, a soft tease,
Carried by the wandering breeze.
Each wave a riddle, deep and wide,
In the ocean's embrace, truths abide.

Secrets swirl in the azure blue,
Waiting for hearts that seek and pursue.
Mysterious tides hold stories grand,
In every drop, the past will stand.

Currents shift with a knowing laugh,
Charting journeys on an unseen path.
With every surge, lessons arise,
In the ocean's gaze, a wise disguise.

From shells and foam, to depths unseen,
Each treasure holds a meaning keen.
As sailors ponder, spirits roam,
In the ocean's embrace, they've found home.

With moonlight casting silver trails,
The sea unveils its ancient tales.
In riddles of the deep, we're bound,
In nature's arms, peace can be found.

Whispers from the Ocean's Embrace

Beneath the waves, a soft voice calls,
Where sunlight breaks and darkness falls.
A melody drifts on currents wide,
Secrets held in the ocean's tide.

Gentle whispers of tales untold,
Echoing dreams of sailors bold.
Each ebb and flow, a story spun,
In the embrace of the waves we run.

Shells like pearls, a treasure found,
Soft sands cradling the ocean's sound.
With each crash, the waters sigh,
Whispers of love that never die.

Stars above in twilight dance,
While deep below, the spirits prance.
In salty air, our worries fade,
By the ocean's touch, we are remade.

In twilight's grace, we find our peace,
A soothing balm that brings us ease.
From ocean's heart, we hear the song,
In whispered waves, we all belong.

Secrets of the Sunken Grove

In shadows deep where silence sleeps,
The sunken grove its secret keeps.
Ancient trees entwined in coral,
Stirring tales from long ago oral.

Time stands still where currents play,
In emerald hues, lost dreams sway.
Each root a story, each branch a sigh,
Of forgotten lives that drifted by.

The waters murmur, a soft refrain,
Of whispered woes and joyous gain.
In this realm, the mysteries roam,
A hidden world, a sunken home.

Lost treasures sleep in silent bows,
While ocean's pulse forever vows.
To guard the secrets, old as time,
In depths unknown, a world sublime.

Through tangled paths of sea and sand,
The grove whispers, a gentle hand.
In its embrace, we find our quest,
To uncover truths, our hearts at rest.

Luminous Tides and Hidden Treasures

Beneath the glow of a silver moon,
The ocean sings a timeless tune.
Tides that glisten, treasures keen,
In the depths, a world unseen.

Waves that crash upon the shore,
Hold secrets of a bygone lore.
With every rise, a story sparks,
In hidden caves, where daylight harks.

A seashell glimmers, whispers near,
Echoes of dreams, both far and near.
Luminous paths where adventures weave,
In the dance of surf, we believe.

Joyful secrets swept by the sea,
In every tide, a mystery.
Glimmers of hope, like stars in the night,
Guide us forth with their radiant light.

So let us dive in waters deep,
Where laughter rings, and shadows sleep.
In luminous tides, we'll sail away,
Chasing treasures that greet the day.

Echoes of the Coral Kingdom

In coral halls where colors bloom,
Lives a kingdom, free from gloom.
With every flicker, a life unfolds,
In vibrant waves, their story told.

The fish dance bright in liquid lace,
In a realm of magic, a sacred space.
Each heartbeat syncs with ocean's sway,
In coral gardens where dreams play.

Tangles of seaweed, a graceful drift,
Nature's art, a precious gift.
The whispers of currents, soft and low,
Guide the wanderers where to go.

A kingdom rich in thrum and pulse,
Where harmony reigns without repulse.
In every corner, a tale appears,
Echoes of joy, and echoes of fears.

Join the dance of the ocean's sheen,
Embrace the beauty, pure and keen.
In the coral kingdom, we shall find,
The rhythms and echoes that bind mankind.

Enchanted Riddles of the Deep

Beneath the waves where shadows play,
Whispers sing of ancient day.
Secrets wrapped in salty mist,
Every crest a hidden twist.

Flickering lights in darkened tide,
Guide the lost with gentle pride.
Creatures dance in velvet night,
Unlocking paths to endless light.

Coral castles, bright and wide,
Guard the dreams the sea will hide.
Each shell holds a tale to share,
Of sunken ships and ghosts laid bare.

Floating treasures, time entwined,
In ocean's grasp, we seek and find.
Every wave a story told,
Of mysteries both new and old.

So dive within the liquid hue,
For every riddle leads to you.
In depths where the heartbeats leap,
Awake the enchantment of the deep.

Luminous Finds in Aquatic Realms

In sapphire depths, a glow appears,
Glimmers born from timeless years.
Jewel-like beings softly sway,
Dancing 'neath the lunar ray.

Crimson reefs and azure skies,
Hold the truth behind our lies.
Nature's palette, rich and bold,
Paints adventures yet untold.

Amongst the kelp, where currents weave,
Secrets linger, few perceive.
Every glance, a hidden prize,
In the deep, the magic lies.

Echoes of a world pristine,
Where vibrant lives and dreams convene.
Bubbles rising in a stream,
Carry whispers of a dream.

So treasure the finds in each domain,
For luminescence hides the pain.
In the realm where water sings,
Beckons forth the joy it brings.

Tranquil Dreams of Oceanic Riches

Drift in currents soft and slow,
Where gentle tides begin to flow.
Peaceful realms of turquoise blue,
Offer solace, tried and true.

Among the sands, soft breath of sea,
Portrays the dreams that long to be.
Seashell whispers, tender grace,
Echoing the ocean's embrace.

Turtles glide through liquid dreams,
In a world where starlight beams.
Every wave a lullaby,
Softly sings as time slips by.

Treasures found in every nook,
Soft the cradles of the brook.
Moments caught, a fleeting kiss,
In the sea's eternal bliss.

So let the ocean's lull unwind,
With tranquil dreams, our hearts aligned.
In depths where serenity lies,
We find our wealth in tranquil skies.

Silken Threads of Submerged Wonders

Silken threads of ocean's weave,
Crafted with the dreams we leave.
Beneath the waves, a tapestry,
Of life and lore in harmony.

Gentle currents, secrets spun,
Shimmer softly in the sun.
Every ripple holds a tale,
Of distant lands and whispered sail.

In watery realms, we intertwine,
Wonders woven, bright and fine.
A dance of colors, bold and bright,
Unfolding visions, pure delight.

Treasures resting 'neath the glimmer,
Where the depths grow ever dimmer.
We find the peace in every thread,
In the stories of the dead.

So let us journey, side by side,
With silken dreams, our hearts abide.
In the ocean's embrace, we roam,
Discovering a place called home.

Chasing Sunlit Reflections

Golden rays dance on the tide,
Beneath the warmth, dreams collide.
Footprints linger in the sand,
As waves whisper, hand in hand.

Seagulls soar with gentle grace,
Nature paints, a fleeting trace.
Clouds drift softly, skies embrace,
Time flows on, a slow-paced race.

The horizon blushes in the night,
Stars awaken, silver light.
In the distance, lanterns glow,
Secrets in the currents flow.

Heartbeats match the ocean's drum,
With every wave, we rise, we come.
Chasing shadows, chasing beams,
In dusk's calm, we share our dreams.

Through the twilight, hopes take flight,
Reflections shimmer, pure delight.
In this dance of light and sea,
We find our place, you and me.

Guardians of the Glistening Depths

Silent watchers in the blue,
Ancient tales known by few.
Every ripple, every swell,
Holds the stories they could tell.

Coral gardens, vibrant hue,
Life teems where currents cue.
Gentle giants glide with pride,
In the depths, they choose to bide.

Through the shadows, journeys start,
Echoes of a beating heart.
Whales sing songs of olden times,
Melodies in liquid rhymes.

Mysteries wrapped in foam and eyes,
Guardians beneath open skies.
In the twilight, creatures dance,
Life unfolds, a hidden chance.

With each tide, they call our name,
Nature's gifts, an endless claim.
In their world, we find our peace,
Guardians of the deep's release.

Songs of the Salty Breeze

Whispers carried through the air,
Salted mist, a dance so rare.
Every breath, a tale unspun,
Underneath the golden sun.

Waves will churn, and shadows play,
Nature's music, night and day.
Seagrass sways, a gentle tune,
Echoes stretch beneath the moon.

The ocean's heart beats strong and free,
Singing songs, eternally.
Tides will pull, the stars will shine,
In their rhythm, we align.

Winds entwine beneath the sky,
Brush of breeze, a soft goodbye.
Nature's canvas, vast and wide,
In its embrace, we will abide.

With each gust, new dreams ignite,
In the salty air, pure delight.
Together, we will roam and seize,
The eternal songs of salty breeze.

The Silver Lace of Ocean Currents

Glistening threads beneath the sea,
Weaving tales of mystery.
In the depths, they twist and flow,
The dance of fate, softly aglow.

Echoes of the waves' soft roar,
Carrying whispers to the shore.
Silver lace in twilight's grasp,
Nature's hand in gentle clasp.

Current's path, an unknown quest,
Guiding dreams to sweetly rest.
Drifting with the tide's embrace,
Finding solace in the space.

Stars above, like lanterns shine,
Lighting trails that intertwine.
In the depths, our spirits soar,
The silver lace forevermore.

As the sea sings its sweet refrain,
We drift softly, free from pain.
In the ocean's timeless swirl,
We find our peace, we find our world.

The Siren's Breath and Glistening Find

Upon the rocks where shadows creep,
A wistful song calls me to sleep.
Lured by the notes, my heart takes flight,
In depths unknown, through day and night.

Siren's breath, a fragrant air,
Weaves through dreams, a spell so rare.
Glistening find, your treasure glows,
In hidden depths where the current flows.

Waves whisper secrets, soft and low,
Each ebb and tide, a tale in tow.
In the twilight, visions blend,
In the ocean's heart, we find our end.

With every pulse, the sea's embrace,
I chase the light, a fleeting trace.
Lost in time, the moments cease,
In the siren's call, I find my peace.

Neptune's Secrets and Ocean's Gifts

Beneath the tides where legends sleep,
Neptune guards the secrets deep.
Wonders await in a coral maze,
Where shadows dance in watery haze.

With every wave, the tales unfold,
In currents warm, in waters cold.
Ocean's gifts, a treasure trove,
In pearls of wisdom, the deep we rove.

Mysterious depths, the abyss calls,
Whispers of time in the ocean sprawl.
Creatures twirl in a graceful waltz,
Every ripple, a soft convulse.

Hidden realms where the sunlight bends,
A world unknown that never ends.
In Neptune's realm, we seek the dawn,
To dance with tides, forever drawn.

Fragile Echoes Among the Waves

In the stillness, echoes play,
Whispers of the ocean sway.
Fragile notes float in the air,
Carried softly, a gentle care.

Among the waves, a heartbeat thrums,
Songs of sailors, lost and numb.
Each pulse a story, every spray,
Memories linger, fade away.

The sea's embrace, both warm and chill,
In liquid dreams, our hearts are still.
Fragments dance in the sun's soft light,
Among the waves, we seek the night.

Tides pull strong, yet softly sigh,
In every swell, a lullaby.
Fragile echoes, a timeless tune,
Lost among stars beneath the moon.

The Dance of Moonlit Ripples

Under the moon, the waters gleam,
A silver stage where shadows beam.
Ripples twist with a soft embrace,
In the night's waltz, we find our place.

Stars reflect in a lover's gaze,
As the ocean sings in a hushed praise.
The dance begins in a rhythmic flow,
Moonlit ripples, a gentle show.

Whispers of night, secrets to keep,
In the depths, where mermaids sleep.
Every wave, a soft caress,
In the moonlight, we find our rest.

Together we move, hearts entwined,
In nature's pulse, our souls aligned.
The dance of ripples, an endless trance,
In the ocean's heart, we take our chance.

The Moon's Dance on Water

The moon casts silver beams,
Rippling paths on quiet streams.
Whispers of the night take flight,
Guiding dreams with soft, pale light.

Waves sparkle like scattered gems,
Each a story in the hems.
The water shimmers, calm and deep,
Where secrets of the night still sleep.

Underneath, the shadows play,
Hidden lives in moonlit sway.
A dance of gentle, ebbing tides,
Where the magic of stillness hides.

As the stars blink in delight,
The world sleeps, cradled tight.
The moon and water's embrace,
A serene, enchanting space.

Nautical Lore of Lost Riches

In the depths where shadows weep,
Treasures lost in secrets deep.
Whispers of a sailor's tale,
Carried forth by wind and sail.

A pirate's map, bloodstained and torn,
Guide to riches, forever worn.
Buried gems on sandy shores,
Guarded by the ocean's roars.

Rusty anchors, ships in gloom,
Echoes of a sailor's doom.
Distant laughter in the breeze,
Fading whispers of the seas.

Legends speak of ghosts at night,
Carved in stone, the lost delight.
Fateful storms that turned the tide,
Stories where romance and danger collide.

Dancers of the Ocean Floor

Beneath the waves, a world unfolds,
In silence, where the beauty holds.
Colors swirl in graceful flows,
A waltz where only the ocean goes.

Coral reefs, a vibrant maze,
Home to life in endless blaze.
Fins flicker like silken threads,
Tales unwritten, where life spreads.

Stars of the sea in gentle glide,
In rhythmic motions, they abide.
Sea turtles twirl in elegant arcs,
In the deep, where no one embarks.

Anemones sway with the tide,
A dance that the currents guide.
Harmony in every breath,
Celebrating life and death.

Guardians of the Aquatic Realms

In the depths, they watch and wait,
Guardians of a watery fate.
Mighty creatures, wise and old,
Protectors of treasures untold.

Leviathans roam in silent grace,
Their ancient wisdom carves the space.
With every ripple, they command,
The rhythm of the ocean's hand.

The ebb and flow, a sacred trust,
In their embrace, we learn to adjust.
Whales sing songs of ages past,
Voices echoing, unsurpassed.

Octopuses weave intricate dreams,
Shadows that dance by moonlight beams.
In every cavern, every reef,
Their watchful eyes weave hope and belief.

Adrift Amongst Glimmering Fantasies

In the twilight's gentle air,
Dreams drift softly, unaware.
Stars above begin to twinkle,
Casting shadows, hearts may crinkle.

Waves embrace the night so bright,
Whispers dance in silver light.
Sailing on a sea of thought,
Finding solace in the sought.

Mirages shimmer, hopes take flight,
A tranquil heart finds pure delight.
Glimmering visions lead the way,
To realms where night transcends to day.

In this realm of sweet escape,
Fantasies in dreams we drape.
No anchor holds, no need for ties,
As starry wonders fill our skies.

A voyage born of light and grace,
Leads each soul to a sacred place.
Adrift we float, no end in sight,
In glimmering fantasies, we ignite.

The Dance of Ocean's Jewels

Beneath the waves, a world unfolds,
jeweled treasures, stories told.
Coral gardens sway and bloom,
In the deep, dispelling gloom.

Fish of colors, bright and rare,
Weave through currents, dance in air.
Morning light begins to spill,
Casting magic, time stands still.

Each tide brings a rhythmic beat,
Nature's music, soft and sweet.
Glimmers flicker, shadows play,
Creating worlds where dreams can sway.

Anemones in vibrant hues,
Ballet dance with ocean blues.
Dolphins leap, the sirens sing,
In harmony, the sea takes wing.

Through whirlpools and gentle swells,
Secrets kept where silence dwells.
The ocean's jewels, wild and free,
Invite us in, just wait and see.

Beneath the Surface of Liquid Dreams

In depths where shadows softly lie,
Ripples whisper, time slips by.
Visions swirl in turquoise deep,
Awakening the soul from sleep.

A gentle current pulls along,
Voices echo an ancient song.
Stars above, through water gleam,
Guiding hearts through fragile dreams.

Mysterious realms beneath the sea,
Where every heart can learn to be.
In the lull of waves that sway,
Hidden truths come out to play.

Colors blend, the mind takes flight,
In liquid depths, it feels so right.
Beneath the surface, we explore,
Endless wonders, evermore.

A journey forged in peace and calm,
Carried by the ocean's balm.
In every loss, there is a gain,
Liquid dreams, where joy remains.

Voyage Through Nautical Mysteries

Underneath the endless sky,
Adventurers set sail and fly.
Charts of stars, the compass glows,
Guiding ships where the ocean flows.

Secrets woven in the tide,
Ancient echoes, the ocean's guide.
Every wave hides stories true,
Of lost kingdoms and skies so blue.

From storms that rage to tranquil nights,
Each nautical path ignites new sights.
Sailing on wind, with hearts ablaze,
Searching for the sun's warm rays.

Beneath the hull, the shadows play,
Watchful spirits call and sway.
Navigating through the dreams we chart,
In every sailor beats a heart.

Through mysteries both dark and bright,
The ocean's depth reveals its light.
A voyage bold, forever free,
In nautical mysteries, we see.

Mystical Bounty of the Briny Abyss

In depths where shadows softly dance,
Secrets whisper, beckoning chance.
Colors shimmer, spirits glide,
Life unfolds in the ocean's tide.

Coral gardens hide their lore,
Echoes of ancient tales in store.
Fishes flash in radiant hues,
A hidden world, where dreams ensue.

With every wave, a story flows,
Of sunken ships and treasures' prose.
Mermaids sing their haunting songs,
In these deep waters, where heart belongs.

Scents of salt and mystery blend,
As the currents twist and bend.
Journey into the ocean's chest,
To unveil nature's wondrous quest.

In this abyss, time stands still,
With every breath, a subtle thrill.
The briny depths, a soothing balm,
In their embrace, life feels like a psalm.

Secrets Hidden in the Waves

Upon the waves, in moonlit glow,
Secrets murmur, ebb and flow.
What lies beneath, unseen by man,
A tale of time, a quiet plan.

The ocean whispers soft and low,
Tales of sailors long ago.
Each ripple brings a cryptic sign,
A world entwined in the divine.

Shells hold secrets, long forgot,
Dreams and wishes, time's knot.
Crabs scuttle, guardians of sand,
In this realm, the lost command.

With every tide, the stories shift,
An endless saga, a precious gift.
The waves embrace, as day departs,
Holding dreams of countless hearts.

Gazing deep, I learn to trust,
In the ocean's realm, it's primed with lust.
For in its depths, we find our race,
Secrets hidden, an endless chase.

Journey Through the Enchanted Blue

Sailing forth on azure seas,
Where dreams abound in the gentle breeze.
The horizon beckons, far and wide,
A voyage of wonder, the heart's guide.

Fish dart by in shimmering trails,
Each splash a testament that never fails.
Beneath the waves, the sirens call,
A magical realm, enchanting all.

Coral castles twist and turn,
In the light, they sparkle and burn.
A journey through this azure frame,
Where every glance sparks a flame.

Drifting softly, I lose my fears,
Finding solace within the spheres.
In the enchanted blue's embrace,
I find a tranquil, sacred space.

With every breath, the ocean sighs,
Echoing dreams beneath vast skies.
A journey marked by the soul's hue,
In the depths of the enchanted blue.

Lure of the Moonlit Seafloor

Beneath the silver, glowing moon,
The seafloor hums a haunting tune.
With every step on shifting sand,
I feel the magic, close at hand.

Corals bathe in ethereal light,
Transforming shadows into vibrant sight.
The lull of waves, a gentle pull,
In this world, my heart is full.

Ebbing tides unveil the past,
Secrets waiting, woven vast.
Whispers echo, soft and clear,
In this realm, I cast away fear.

Dance of stars above me glows,
As the ocean whispers timeless prose.
The lure of depths, a sweet embrace,
In moonlit waters, I find my place.

Together, we drift, heart in hand,
Finding freedom in sea and sand.
As night unfolds, the magic swells,
Beneath the moon, all mystery dwells.

Echoing Lullabies of the Tide

Soft whispers dance on waves,
Cuddled dreams in moonlit caves.
Stars align with soothing grace,
Time slows down in this embrace.

Seashell songs of night's delight,
Carry hearts on sails of light.
Every ripple tells a tale,
Of gentle winds that softly sail.

The ocean hums a tender tune,
Cradled 'neath the watchful moon.
Ebb and flow, a serenade,
In salty air, sweet memories made.

In dreams we find our solace here,
The tide's caress, so warm and near.
With every pulse, the heartbeats bind,
In echoing lullabies, we're combined.

Thy rhythm sways with nature's grace,
Time enshrined in this vast space.
Embraced by night, we drift away,
As lullabies, the waves do play.

Whimsical Currents and Submerged Identities

Beneath the waves, a world unseen,
Whirls of colors, vibrant and keen.
Currents twist with secrets held,
In aquatic realms, our souls are melded.

Mirrors shimmering in the waves,
Reflecting dreams that the sea braves.
Faces change like tides that roll,
Seeking treasures that speak to the soul.

With every flicker of the light,
New identities emerge in flight.
Playful fish in hues so bright,
Dance in shadows, a wondrous sight.

In depths where time and thought entwine,
The essence of who we are will shine.
Embrace the whims of currents bold,
In submerged worlds, our stories unfold.

We dive into the unknown vast,
Leaving behind the land, the past.
Drifting where the wild waves call,
In whimsical currents, we find our all.

Mysterious Beckon of the Deep

A siren's song beckons at dusk,
Echoes hauntingly, a perfumed musk.
Drawing us close to abyssal dreams,
Where light fades and reality seems.

Whispers swirl in the darkened blue,
Secrets linger in shadows anew.
Each heartbeat calls with a velvet sigh,
As tides embrace, our spirits fly.

The pulse of the ocean sings low,
Beneath the surface, mysteries flow.
Ancient tales of ship and star,
In solitude, we wander far.

Awash in an ocean of silent dread,
Visions dance of what once was said.
Caught in the current, we feel the pull,
Mysterious beckon, both dark and cool.

Deep down the soul's yearning swims,
In the shadows where beauty dims.
Yet from the depths, a light shall rise,
Wrapped in the ocean's endless ties.

A Mazed Path of Enchantment

Winding trails through emerald seas,
Where dreams waltz on the evening breeze.
Each step leads to realms unknown,
In nature's maze, our hearts have grown.

Crystal waters and glimmering light,
Guide our journey through day and night.
Every twist, a new surprise,
In the enchanted, we seek the wise.

Lush foliage sways with secrets shared,
Echoes of laughter, the heart bared.
With every turn, magic unfolds,
In this path, our story molds.

Stars twinkle down through leafy bends,
As the night whispers, our journey blends.
In a maze adorned with fates entwined,
We wander on, forever aligned.

Let the path lead where it may,
With faith in the magic, we shall stay.
In a mazed realm, we find our kin,
And lose ourselves, yet always win.

Treasures of the Tidal Depths

In the depths where the shadows play,
Glistening pearls in the soft clay.
Ancient shipwrecks sing their song,
Guarding secrets that linger long.

Colorful fishes, darting bright,
Dance like stars in the deep blue night.
Jewel-toned corals, a vibrant scene,
Nature's bounty, pure and serene.

Whispers of waves, a soothing sound,
Legends and lore forever abound.
Hidden treasures beneath each wave,
In the ocean's embrace, we are brave.

Tides that ebb with a gentle grace,
Finding joy in this watery place.
Crabs and shells in the golden sand,
Together, forming a wondrous land.

Beneath the surface, a world unseen,
In the heart of the ocean, pure and clean.
Each ripple tells a story anew,
Treasures found in the ocean's blue.

Whispered Secrets of the Sea

Morning light on the ocean's crest,
Whispers drifting, a tranquil nest.
Tales of sailors long since passed,
Echo softly, the die is cast.

Secrets linger where shadows fall,
In the currents, they speak to all.
Waves carrying dreams from afar,
Sailing onward, chasing a star.

Bubbles rising, gentle and slow,
Revealing depths we long to know.
Messages written in the sands,
In every grain, the heart understands.

Tides of longing, tides of peace,
In their rhythm, our worries cease.
Listen closely, let your heart sway,
To the whispers of the sea today.

Dreams suspended on a silver line,
In the ocean's heart, our souls entwine.
Secrets exchanged in the moonlit foam,
In each wave's sigh, we find a home.

Shimmering Gems in Coral Caves

Deep in the reef where colors bloom,
Gems of the ocean dispel all gloom.
Coral gardens, lush and bright,
A hidden world under soft twilight.

Fish like rainbows dart through the frame,
In these caves, every life has a name.
Echoing currents whisper and play,
Guiding the lost on their way.

Tidal treasures in every nook,
Ancient stories in every look.
From the depths, a soft voice calls,
An invitation where magic befalls.

Crystals glimmer with each passing tide,
Welcoming all who wish to glide.
In the embrace of the coral's sway,
Dreams and wonders dance and play.

In this realm where the sea meets land,
Nature's artistry, perfectly planned.
Shimmering gems in caverns roam,
In these coral caves, we find our home.

Echoes of the Ocean's Heart

In the silence where waves retreat,
Echoes murmur, a heartbeat's beat.
Songs of sailors from times long gone,
Harmonizing with the breaking dawn.

Deep beneath where the sunbeams fade,
Whispers of secrets, softly laid.
The ocean's heart, both fierce and kind,
In every pulse, a truth we find.

Currents dance with a knowing grace,
Tracing patterns as time does race.
From the depths, a soft, sweet sigh,
Fills the world where dreams can fly.

Glistening tides wash over the shore,
Opening windows to ancient lore.
The sea reflects our hopes and fears,
Cradling life throughout the years.

As the moon beckons the waves to rise,
In its glow, our spirits prize.
The echoes of the ocean's stay,
Guide us gently, come what may.

Celestial Wonders in Brine

Stars dance above the ocean's edge,
Whispers of the tide softly pledge.
Moonlight kisses waves with grace,
As dreams drift in the salt-tinged space.

Shells hold stories, long concealed,
Secrets of the sea revealed.
Glistening treasures in the night,
Hold the cosmos, pure delight.

Whirlpools spin in cosmic flight,
Reflecting worlds bathed in light.
With every crest, a wish takes form,
In briny depths, life's vibrant storm.

Waves like lullabies gently rise,
In a dance beneath the skies.
Each drop a tale, each tide a song,
In the ocean's heart, we belong.

Where water meets the stars so bright,
Celestial wonders in the night.
In every breath of salty air,
The universe dreams, free as a prayer.

Melodies of Forgotten Waters

Ripples sing of days gone by,
Lost in the soft lullaby.
Echoes linger where waters weave,
Secrets held that we believe.

Fading dreams in the twilight dim,
Dance around on the water's rim.
Songs of silence ripple through,
Whispers of the deep, so true.

Old boats rock on memories' tide,
Carrying hearts where hopes reside.
Beneath the surface, stories wait,
Melodies of time, we celebrate.

Each wave a note, each splash a line,
Creating music, so divine.
Across the ages, hear them play,
Forgotten waters, lost today.

Shadows move with the evening breeze,
Nature's chorus among the trees.
In every corner, notes align,
Melodies that forever shine.

The Treasures that Time Keeps

In the depths of ocean's hold,
Countless stories left untold.
Corals bloom like ancient scripts,
Wisdom in the sea, it drips.

Beneath the waves, a world unseen,
Where time stands still, and soul can glean.
Each grain of sand holds history,
Whispers of the sea's mystery.

From shipwrecks lost, and pearls that gleam,
Items of a long-lost dream.
Glistening jewels of the past,
In watery graves, forever cast.

Time unfolds in the ocean's embrace,
Holding treasures that we chase.
Fleeting glimpses of life confined,
In watery depths, all intertwined.

Erosion teaches through gentle strife,
In nature's rhythm, the pulse of life.
Each moment a treasure, each wave a sweep,
In the heart of the ocean, secrets keep.

Shadows of Sparkling Waters

Under the moonlit, shimmering tides,
Shadows whisper, where the stillness hides.
Reflections dance with the gentle night,
As stars cascade, a delicate light.

Silhouettes sway beneath the tide,
In the twilight, shadows reside.
Stories woven in the stream,
Ebb and flow of a timeless dream.

Glimmers flicker on the rippling glass,
A moment's pause, as time does pass.
In watery depths where secrets lie,
Shadows flutter, a soft sigh.

Echoes of laughter, whispers of pain,
Each ripple tells of joy and rain.
On the surface, a sparkling gleam,
Beneath, a world that weaves and teems.

From dusk till dawn, the waters play,
Casting shadows that drift away.
In every wave, a memory stirs,
Where shadows and shimmering waters blur.

Mysteries in the Blue Abyss

In shadows deep where silence lies,
A world unfolds beneath the skies.
Whispers call from depths unknown,
Secrets held in water's throne.

Strange creatures dance in swirling twirls,
Twinkling lights like hidden pearls.
Echoes ripple through the night,
Shrouded tales of ancient might.

Caverns dark with treasures rare,
Silent watchers in their lair.
Legends drift on currents free,
Tides that weave their mystery.

Glimmering surface, a world above,
Below, a realm of endless love.
The abyss hums a haunting tune,
In the deep, where dreams are strewn.

In the blue, where shadows play,
The ocean's heart will guide the way.
To wander souls who seek to find,
The enigmas left behind.

Glimmers of the Ocean's Heart

The sun breaks through the water's skin,
Casting light where journeys begin.
Gentle waves in a soft embrace,
Harbor whispers of distant grace.

Colors dance like painted dreams,
Reflecting sunbeams in silver streams.
The ocean's heart beats strong and clear,
In every splash, a story near.

Secrets hidden in sandy beds,
Tales of sailors, long since fled.
Glimmers call from a world apart,
Echoes of the ocean's heart.

Starlit nights and tidal plays,
New horizons in twilight's haze.
A journey beckons, wide and vast,
To find the treasures of the past.

In the depths, where wonders lie,
The glimmers draw our curious eye.
To touch the soul of seas profound,
In the ocean's heart, we're forever bound.

Secrets in the Shell's Embrace

Cradled softly in ancient shells,
Lie whispered truths, where silence dwells.
Each curve and line, a story spun,
The dance of life, a race well-run.

A gleaming world in layers tight,
Where secrets hide from grasping light.
The ocean's songs, both sweet and bold,
In every shell, a tale retold.

Listen close to the fragile sound,
Of hidden worlds that swirl around.
Embraced by the tide's gentle kiss,
In shells we find our ocean's bliss.

A treasure trove of memory,
In every shell, a legacy.
Waves may shift, yet still they stay,
Guarding secrets lost in spray.

Through seashell doors, we drift and roam,
In the ocean's heart, we find our home.
With each discovery, we reclaim,
The secrets whispered in their name.

Sylphs and the Shimmering Depths

In azure realms where spirits gleam,
Sylphs frolic in a liquid dream.
With laughter bright, they weave the night,
In the depths where wonders ignite.

Seas like glass reflect their grace,
Each movement, a dance in a timeless space.
Whispers of currents flow like air,
Sylphs spin tales through waters rare.

Air and sea in harmony blend,
In shimmering depths where questions end.
A waltz of waves, a gentle sigh,
Echoes of myths that never die.

Glistening scales of creatures old,
Guard the dreams that they unfold.
In brine-soaked realms, a magic stirs,
Life and myth, their spirit purrs.

Through sapphire skies and coral reefs,
Sylphs guide the hearts of wandering leaves.
To journey far, where few have gone,
In shimmering depths, our souls are drawn.

Shades of Calm on the Deep Blue

Beneath the sky, vast dreams unwind,
Gentle waves cradle thoughts so kind.
Whispers of peace in every crest,
Serenity flows, a tranquil nest.

Horizon calls with colors bright,
The sun dips low, embracing night.
Soft reflections dance on the tide,
Where the heart finds joy to bide.

Clouds drift by like cotton dreams,
The ocean speaks in soothing themes.
Every ripple holds a story,
In the depths, we seek our glory.

Anchored hope in waters deep,
Promises made that we must keep.
In shades of calm, we find our truth,
Moments captured, reclaimed youth.

From azure depths, the spirit sings,
A melody that nature brings.
In this embrace, our worries cease,
Shades of calm provide us peace.

Enigmatic Whispers from Below

In the depths, secrets softly dwell,
Ancient tales, the ocean's swell.
Mysteries wrapped in the ocean's blue,
Echoes of life, both old and new.

Silhouettes glide in shadows deep,
Guardians of dreams, their watch they keep.
Bubbles rise, like laughter heard,
Enigmatic whispers without a word.

Serpents curl in seaweed weave,
Through shifting sands, they twist and cleave.
From coral homes, they often stray,
Dancing gently in twilight's play.

A world unknown beneath the wave,
Bold adventures for the brave.
Yet stillness reigns in every flow,
Enigmatic whispers call us low.

In twilight's glow, our souls connect,
Finding beauty in the wrecked.
The ocean's song, forever binds,
Enigmatic whispers, hearts aligned.

Lullabies of the Ocean's Pulse

Cradled by the rhythmic swells,
Where the ocean's heartbeat dwells.
Gentle lullabies softly sung,
In every wave, our hearts are strung.

Moonlit dances across the bay,
Guiding dreams to drift away.
Serenade of the sea so vast,
In its arms, we find the past.

Salt and breeze, a sweet embrace,
Whispers of time, a sacred space.
The pulse of water, deep and strong,
A soothing hymn that lasts lifelong.

In twilight's grip, the stars align,
Illuminated paths divine.
With every breath, the ocean sighs,
Lullabies beneath the skies.

Resting safe in the drifting tide,
With open hearts, we turn the ride.
In nature's cradle, softly we rest,
Lullabies of the ocean's best.

Rippled Jewels of Sunkissed Existence

Glimmers dance on the water's face,
Sunkissed treasures in endless space.
Each ripple tells a tale untold,
Jewels of life, both bright and bold.

In the shallows, colors collide,
Nature's palette, a vibrant tide.
Shells and stones, a story spun,
Rippled jewels beneath the sun.

With every wave, a heartbeat shared,
Moments cherished, hearts laid bare.
In this glittering, golden sea,
Existence sparkles, wild and free.

The sun will rise; the tides will change,
Yet amidst it all, hearts rearrange.
In symphony with nature's song,
Rippled jewels where we belong.

From shore to shore, our souls shall roam,
In this vast ocean, we find our home.
Each moment glistens in life's embrace,
Rippled jewels of timeless grace.

A Glimmer in the Ocean's Lament

Beneath the waves, a whisper glows,
Secrets of the tide in quiet flows.
Each shimmer tells a tale untold,
Of journeys lost and myths of old.

The moonlight dances on the crest,
While shadows cradle nature's jest.
A glimmer sparks in depths so deep,
Where dreams of sailors softly sleep.

The currents sigh a sorrowed tune,
Embracing echoes of the moon.
In salty tears, the memories dwell,
Of shipwrecks, and the ocean's spell.

Each cresting wave, a fleeting chance,
To witness time's aquatic dance.
A glimmer fades, then reappears,
As ocean's heart reveals its fears.

So listen close to ocean's call,
For every whisper tells us all.
In depths where shadows weave and wend,
A glimmer shines beyond the end.

Songs Held by the Deep's Embrace

In depths so dark, a melody,
Awakens songs of mystery.
Held by the sea in softest clasp,
Where echoes dance and memories grasp.

The whales' refrain and dolphins' cheer,
Resound like whispers, crystal clear.
A symphony of currents flows,
In every wave, a story grows.

From coral caves where shadows play,
To sunlit reefs where colors sway.
The deep holds secrets in its space,
A tapestry of time and grace.

Each note dissolves in salty air,
As sailors listen, unaware.
For in the depths, the songs remain,
A chorus of love, loss, and gain.

So heed the songs and let them guide,
As we embrace the ocean wide.
In every tide, a world unfolds,
Through melodies that never grow old.

A Tidal Canvas of Secrets

The sea paints stories on the shore,
With every wave, a tale to explore.
A canvas vast, of blue and gold,
Where whispers of the past unfold.

Each grain of sand holds echoes near,
Of ancient mariners who steered clear.
Their dreams still dance on rippling crest,
In tidal rhythms, they find rest.

Secrets held beneath the foam,
Invisible threads that call them home.
Brushstrokes of storms and calm collide,
In nature's art, where mysteries hide.

A tide may ebb, yet still it flows,
With every pulse, its heartbeat glows.
From dusk to dawn, it will embrace,
The silent stories time can trace.

So wander where the waters meet,
And listen to the ocean's beat.
A tidal tale, forever spun,
Where art and life forever run.

The Murmur of Aquatic Fantasies

In the twilight's soft embrace,
The water whispers, leaves no trace.
A murmur rising from the deep,
Where dreams and secrets softly creep.

Bubbles rise like fleeting thoughts,
Of stories woven, battles fought.
Each ripple breathes a ghostly lore,
From ancient depths to distant shore.

Mermaids sing in haunting tones,
Beneath the waves, their hearts like stones.
In currents swift, they laugh and wail,
Carving paths through the ocean's veil.

The shadows dance in liquid light,
Where fantasies take graceful flight.
Each ebbing tide, a soft caress,
Revealing depths we can't assess.

So heed the murmur's soft refrain,
For in each wave, there's joy and pain.
With every tide, new dreams arise,
In aquatic worlds beneath the skies.

Starlit Wishes from the Water's Edge

Beneath the sky so wide and bright,
We cast our dreams into the night.
The waves whisper soft and low,
As starlit wishes start to flow.

Each spark above, a hope untold,
In silver hues, our hearts are bold.
The shore embraces dreams like these,
In the night's soft, gentle breeze.

The horizon shimmers, full of grace,
Reflected light in this sacred place.
With every tide, our hopes align,
As starlit wishes intertwine.

We chase the glow of morning light,
Where dreams and water share their flight.
Together they dance, wild and free,
In the heart of the endless sea.

The Ocean's Breath and Radiant Findings

From depths unknown, the ocean sighs,
With secrets held beneath the guise.
Waves crash softly on the shore,
Each breath a tale, a timeless lore.

With every tide, the treasures reveal,
Fragments of dreams that time can't steal.
Radiant findings in sandy beds,
Whispers of stories that nature spreads.

A shell, a stone, a myriad hue,
Each piece a memory, ancient and new.
The ocean sings in rhythm and rhyme,
A melody woven through sands of time.

As dusk descends, the stars ignite,
Guiding souls with their gentle light.
The ocean's breath, a lullaby sweet,
Carries our hopes on waves that greet.

Liquid Dreams of the Sea's Heart

In the depths where dreams reside,
Liquid visions swirl, and glide.
A dance of light, a whispered tune,
Echoing softly beneath the moon.

Sapphire waters cradle the night,
Holding shadows, draped in light.
Bubbles burst with stories told,
Each wave a memory, brave and bold.

In this realm, our spirits soar,
Liquid dreams that we explore.
The sea's heart beats in sync with ours,
Underneath the stars' wide hours.

With every splash, a new regret,
Yet hope afloat, we won't forget.
For in these waters, we find our peace,
As liquid dreams and troubles cease.

Flickering Lights in the Midnight Blue

In midnight blue, the stars arise,
Flickering lights in velvet skies.
The world below, a silent hum,
As whispers of dreams begin to come.

Ripples dance on the water's face,
Mirroring the cosmos' grace.
Each light above, with secrets bright,
Guiding hearts through endless night.

In the stillness, thoughts take flight,
Chasing shadows, seeking light.
With every flicker, hopes entwine,
A tapestry woven, bold and fine.

As dawn approaches, dreams embrace,
The shimmering glow, a warm embrace.
Together we rise with morning's hue,
From flickering lights in the midnight blue.

The Artistry of Salt and Sand

Waves dance upon the shore,
Painting dreams forevermore.
Footprints trace a fleeting path,
A tapestry of nature's wrath.

Seagulls cry, the sun's soft glow,
Whispers of the ocean flow.
Crafting castles, tall and grand,
Built with care from salt and sand.

The tide reveals the shells of yore,
Stories etched in ocean's core.
Each grain of sand, a tale unwinds,
Revealing secrets time confines.

Breezes bring the scent of sea,
In every breath, wild and free.
Nature's palette, vast and wide,
In salt and sand, the world resides.

As twilight falls, the stars ignite,
Guiding dreams through endless night.
The artistry of land and sea,
A canvas rich with memory.

Enchanted Echoes from the Abyss

Deep below the surface blue,
Where light diminishes, fades from view.
Echos of whispers, soft and clear,
Songs of the deep, for none to hear.

Coral gardens, bright and alive,
In shadows where the lost ones thrive.
Creatures dance in a ghostly light,
In the abyss, they own the night.

Mysteries weave through currents strong,
Where time and tide both play along.
Ancient secrets the waters keep,
Hidden tales in darkness, deep.

Strange and wondrous forms emerge,
In a world where dreams converge.
From depths of silence, life does soar,
Echoes linger—forevermore.

As we reach to touch the tide,
The ocean's heart, our souls collide.
Enchanted echoes call us near,
To the abyss, where nothing's clear.

Mystical Waters and Divine Reflections

Rippling waters, calm and bright,
Reflecting dreams in purest light.
Stillness breathing, whispers soft,
The dance of clouds, where shadows loft.

Golden ripples kissed by the sun,
A sacred space where all is one.
Waves that carry tales untold,
In every splash, a secret gold.

Mirrored skies and gentle breeze,
Nature's canvas, intended to please.
Mountains cradle, valleys sigh,
As tears of joy slip from the sky.

Through tranquil depths, where silence reigns,
The chorus of life in gentle chains.
Awakening spirits, we embark,
On journeys deep, through light and dark.

With every wave, a story sings,
Binding us to these ancient things.
In mystical waters, we find grace,
Divine reflections, our sacred place.

Tales from the Nautical Midnight

Beneath the starry, boundless sea,
Whispers of tales call out to me.
Shipwrecked dreams and faded maps,
Echo through the midnight laps.

Moonlit paths on waters wide,
Ghostly sails where shadows glide.
Mariners of old, their spirits roam,
Guiding lost souls back to home.

In the hidden depths they dwell,
Guardians of each ocean's spell.
Stories woven in the tide,
Brought to life where legends hide.

Crimson skies give way to night,
While lanterns flicker, casting light.
The breeze sings songs of ages past,
In nautical midnight, memories last.

With every rise and every fall,
The sea forever tells its call.
Tales from depths where dreams reside,
In midnight's arms, we drift and glide.

Shining Hopes in Marine Shadows

In depths where sunlight sighs,
The whispers of dreams arise.
Creatures dance in twilight's glow,
Guided by the tides that flow.

Shadows weave through coral lanes,
Each heartbeat sings of secret gains.
Hope glimmers in the ocean's breath,
Life thrives despite the chill of death.

Beneath the waves, we find our way,
In muted hues of blue and gray.
A treasure lies in every tear,
For shadows cast can still bring cheer.

With each new tide, we dare to dream,
To rise above and burst the seam.
In silence, strength begins to build,
As ocean's soul becomes fulfilled.

Embracing all that darkness hides,
In watery realms where wonder bides.
Shining hopes like stars take flight,
Unfurling truths beneath the light.

The Quest for Ocean's Heart

Upon the waves, I set my sail,
In search of love, not bound to fail.
The ocean calls with siren song,
A journey vast, where I belong.

Through storms and calm, my spirit sails,
To find the heart where magic prevails.
In depths unknown, I chase the dream,
The light that dances on each beam.

Tides of time and space collide,
In swirling currents, I must abide.
Each wave a story, each swell a start,
Guiding me to ocean's heart.

With every stroke, hope's fire ignites,
A beacon bright in ocean's nights.
The compass leads to purest grace,
As waves embrace my longing face.

At last, I find the buried truth,
In depths that held my heart's own youth.
To love the sea, and all its art,
What more could bless the sailor's heart?

Reflections on the Seafloor's Canvas

Beneath the waves, a world unfolds,
In painted hues, the story's told.
Coral gardens, vibrant and bright,
Reflecting glory in the night.

Each grain of sand, a whispered tale,
Of life that sways, of currents' gale.
In quiet depths, the colors blend,
A masterpiece that has no end.

Light filters down, a shimmering dance,
Where shadows play in a timeless trance.
The seafloor holds a canvas vast,
With every wave, a memory cast.

Life's artistry in every phase,
In shifting sands, the beauty stays.
Reflections shimmer, a dance of fate,
As the ocean's heart, we celebrate.

In this deep realm, serenity lies,
A gentle peace beneath blue skies.
The seafloor's canvas, forever grand,
Nature's brush strokes, a guiding hand.

A Symphony of Celestial Currents

Listen close to the ocean's tune,
A symphony beneath the moon.
The currents rise and ebb with grace,
In harmony, they find their place.

Each wave a note, each tide a beat,
The sea's embrace makes life complete.
A melody of salt and spray,
Where whispers of the deep hold sway.

In every crash upon the shore,
The echoes of the ocean's lore.
A song of stars, a gentle breeze,
Melodic flows that aim to please.

From surface wind to seafloor's hush,
The rhythm moves, a constant rush.
With every swell, the world awakes,
A dance of life that never breaks.

In twilight's glow, the waters sing,
A timeless call, the heart's own ring.
Through cosmic waves, we find our part,
In this grand symphony, love's art.

A Tapestry of Tidal Whispers

In the moon's soft glow, waves weave tales,
Whispers of secrets, where silence pales.
Stars dip their toes in a liquid night,
Each swell a story, each shimmer a light.

Coral blooms dance, vibrant and bright,
As currents hug shores, embracing the night.
The ocean's heart beats, a timeless tune,
Echoes of joy beneath the bright moon.

Shells cradle memories, lost and found,
Each grain of sand holds a whispering sound.
Together they murmur, in unity strong,
A tapestry spun, where all belong.

Enchanted Reflections in the Deep

Beneath the waves, where shadows play,
Reflections shimmer, drifting away.
Mysteries linger in the watery dusk,
Enchantment lingers, in silence we trust.

Fins trace the surface, a dance so divine,
Colors blend softly, like aged fine wine.
Creatures glide gently, in a world so serene,
Their grace unveils the hidden unseen.

Ripples of stories, they whisper in light,
Of journeys untold, in the depths of the night.
Each bubble that rises, a dream to behold,
Tales of the deep, in reflections of gold.

Allure of the Crystal Waters

Crystal waters glisten, pure and alive,
With depths that beckon, where wonders thrive.
Fish dart like jewels, in a ballet so free,
Nature's own canvas, an art to see.

Sunlight caresses every wave's gentle crest,
A symphony echoing, nature's behest.
The pulse of the ocean, reassuring and slow,
Calls to the wanderer, the seeker to go.

In each tide's embrace, we find peace anew,
A sanctuary fleeting, yet ever so true.
With sights and with sounds, all senses alive,
The allure of these waters makes the spirit thrive.

Songs of the Deep-Sea Dreams

In depths where the sunlight dares not tread,
Songs of the deep are sweetly said.
Whales weave ballads, ancient and wise,
Carried on currents, to the vast, open skies.

Echoes of laughter, from gardens below,
With each gentle wave, their joy starts to flow.
Creatures unseen, in shadows they dwell,
Whisper their secrets, a magical spell.

Bubbles rise softly, like laughter in air,
Tales of the ocean, so wondrously rare.
In dreams of the deep, we'll find our own way,
To dance with the rhythm of a saltwater play.